C000000640

Remarks on the Controversy Between Dr. Hawker and Mr. Porter, Concerning the Divinity of Christ, and the Veracity of the Scriptures; in Which the Incompetency of Mr. Porter in the Argument is Proved in Several Instances,

REMARKS

ON THE

CONTROVERSY

BETWEEN

Dr. HAWKER

AND

Mr. PORTER,

CONCERNING

The DIVINITY of CHRIST,

AND

THE VERACITY OF THE SCRIPTURES;

IN WHICH

The Incompetency of Mr. *Porter* in the Argument

IS PROVED IN SEVERAL INSTANCES,

AND

THE TRUTH, PURITY, AND INTEGRITY OF THEM

ARE DEFENDED

Againſt the ASSERTIONS of Mr. PORTER,

WHO AFFIRMS,

"THAT SOME PARTS OF THEM HAVE BEEN DEMONSTRATED TO BE FALSE."

Search the Scriptures, (the Hebrew Scriptures) *for in them ye think ye have eternal life, and they are which teſtify of me.* John v. 39.

PLYMOUTH:

Printed and Sold by P. NETTLETON, No 52, Market-Street; Sold alſo by Mr. J DEIGHTON, No. 325. Holborn, London; Meſſrs. RICHARDS, BARNIKEL, and WILLS, Bookſellers, in Plymouth, Meſſrs. HOXLAND, FRASER, and HEYDON, Bookſellers, Plymouth-Dock, and Mr. WOOLMER, Bookſeller, Exeter.

Price ONE SHILLING.

ADVERTISEMENT.

AS I am accuſtomed to take notes on what I read which I think to be of conſequence; ſo, on peruſing Dr. *Hawker's* Sermons, and Mr. *Porter's* Obſervations on them, I made the following Remarks—which lay by, without a deſign of publiſhing them; till Mr. *Porter* printed and publiſhed a ſecond reply to Dr. *Hawker*, and therein continued his obſervations on what he calls *untruths in the ſcriptures*. On this I thought it my duty, as a believer in Chriſt and the ſcriptures, to publiſh theſe remarks, hoping they may be of ſome uſe in defending the ſacred writings againſt the calumnies thrown on them and our Saviour Jeſus Chriſt.——— At the ſame time I aſſure both Dr. *Hawker* and Mr. *Porter* with the greateſt truth, that I profeſs impartiality to both, and that nothing in the following remarks are deſigned perſonally to either, any further than their different writings have affected me, as one who believes the Revelation of God, and hath Faith in Chriſt.—I do not ſo much as know Mr. *Porter!*—It would give me great pleaſure to do any good office to either,—therefore after this candid profeſſion, I hope, nothing I have wrote will be taken perſonally. The whole deſign of publiſhing the following ſtrictures is to *do my duty* and *openly to confeſs* my belief in the revelation of God, and my Redeemer Jeſus Chriſt.

VERITAS.

REMARKS, &c.

CHAP. I.

On Mr. *Porter's* Defence of Unitarianifm.

SOON after Dr. *Hawker* publifhed his Sermons on the Divinity of Chrift, I read them with great attention, and hoped that they might be a means of doing good, by the inftruction they contained; particularly in the neighbourhood he lived, as many were there who wanted information on that point.

At the firft reading, I wifhed Dr. *Hawker* had alfo brought forward the additional evidence of the Divinity of Chrift from the early writers of the Church, but fince reading Mr. *Porter's* Defence of Unitarianifm, I am well fatisfied that their teftimony would have no weight, but have been a means of increafing and confounding the controverfy; for the Evidence of the Fathers will have but little influence with a man who denies the teftimony of Scripture, and can only tend to prolong and confufe.

I did imagine Dr. *Hawker's* Liberality and Charity *to all* would have prevented an attack from any—however I was miftaken. *Unitarianifm* was affected

by

by what he had written! Soon after I faw an ad-
vertifement mentioning that an Anfwer to Dr.
Hawker in Defence of *Unitarianifm*, by Mr. *Porter*,
was in the prefs. As foon as I procured a copy of
it, I obferved that he agreed to join iffue with Dr.
Hawker on the authority of the fcriptures. By this
conceffion I hoped the Divinity of Chrift would be
determined by them; but how was I difappointed,
when I found, on reading the Defence, that, inftead
of his opinions being determined by fcripture; what
was fcripture was to be determined by Mr. *Porter*
and *his Reafon*. But who can know any thing of
God, but what God himfelf has revealed!

That I may not interrupt the obfervations I have
to make on Mr. *Porter*'s Defence, I fhall throw, in a
note below, a few quotations from his work, to fhew
the method he purfues to get rid of many of the
texts of fcripture which Dr. *Hawker* brought to
prove the Deity of Chrift.

The

ᵛ He begins with afferting " that were we to underftand the Scriptures in a literal fenfe, (as *take, eat,* &c) we fhould *reject with Abhorrence*—and alfo Jofh. x. 13 has been *determined to be falfe*."—
Without troubling the reader with the texts I fhall only mention his
obfervations on them. " (P. 38.) This paffage *(fays he)* does not
" appear *to me* to relate either to the Divinity or pre-exiftence of Chrift.
" (48) Inftead of any Englifh tranflation on John i, 14. and Rom. viii.
" 3. he gives a tranflation, " which is *moft probably* the true one."—
" On Hebrews i. 8. fays, " Inftead of making *worlds*, it fhould be
" that he made *ages*." (51) " With equal propriety it may be render-
" ed different." (58) on Heb. iii. 4. " *Perhaps* the following will be

The quotations as below noticed will fhew us in what manner he is willing this controverfy fhall be decided by fcripture—that is (as the quotations plainly prove) after he has difcarded what parts he pleafes of it, as falfe, and amended the reft, according to his own comprehenfive *reafon.*—By taking this freedom with every part of the fcriptures of the New Teftament he finds no difficulty (as well he cannot) to get rid of any thing he diflikes.

After

" the true interpretation." " *Throughout the Old Teftament but* ONE
" *Being is mentioned* as the creator and preferver of the world; this
" Being is *uniformly* fpoken of as ONE perfon , and is faid to have
" made the world immediately by himfelf, as Gen. i. 1. &c." (64) I
" will now proceed to give what *appears to me* to be the true interpre-
" tration, (66) it is *highly probable* that Jefus Chrift is an interpola-
" tion. (72) on 1 Cor x. 9. " It is *highly probable* our reading is not
" the true one (74) on John xii. 4. It is not *abfolutely certain* that
" the common reading is the true one. (83) Ifa. vii. 14. Behold a
" *Virgin* fhall, &c. and applied by Matthew i. 22, 23. *does not denote*
" that the child who was born of Mary was God."——This is a more
audacious affertion than ever I heard came from the Jews !——(84)
" *More properly* a mighty God. (97) Matth. xviii. 20. This mean-
" ing *poffibly might be.* (101) *It appears* that the true reading of this
" verfe is (105) John xix. 37. we *feem warranted in concluding that*
" *there has been fome miftake.* Tit. ii. 13. Mr. Porter fays *has inter-*
" *pretation* is *more agreeable* to the whole tenor of the fcripture, on
" Tit. i. 3. but *fomewhat more is requifite* to make us believe that the
" Apoftle here intended Jefus Chrift. (109) On a fuppofition this is
" the true reading (110) he tells us that this reading of his (which is
" contrary to what we have in the Bible) gives a *beautiful fenfe.* (151)
" John xx. 28. My Lord and my God! Thefe words, fays he, *may*
" *have* this interpretation. Acts vi. 19. " the true reading is" (156)
" the words may *be rendered* with great propriety."

After endeavouring to deftroy the proofs of the Deity of Chrift by perverting thofe texts of fcripture to his purpofe, Mr. *Porter* brings a number of paf-fages from the New Teftament to prove that Chrift was man.

We believe, as well as Mr. *Porter*, that Chrift was man, of *the feed of the woman (only)* and born of *the Virgin*, which according to the Prophet *Ijaiah*,‡ was to be *the fign* given of his coming in the flefh, and to which *fign* no other man ever had a claim ; this was the *woman's feed* who was to bruife the ferpent's head ! But we do not believe with Mr. *Porter* that he was *mere man* !---We believe that Chrift in his nature was *both God and man*, but ONE Chrift ! therefore he had no occafion to bring fo many texts to prove that he was man ; neither had he occafion to afk, " was it God who fuffered and was crucified? " was it God who had his fide pierced, and cried " out in the agony of death, *my God, my God*, why " haft thou forfaken me ?"---No,---it was Chrift, in his human nature, man, when his God left the man-hood to fuffer *to expiate* the *fin of Adam*, and his po-fterity ; and by his refurrection to affure a new and glorious life, after death, to all thofe who believed the revelation of God, and had a true *faith* in him, for as St. Paul tell us,† *as in Adam all die, even fo in Chrift fhall all be made alive, the firft Adam was made a*
living

---

‡ Ifa. vii. 14.   † 1 Cor. xv. 22.

living soul, the last Adam was made a quickening spirit, who shall change our vile bodies like unto his glorious body *

It was the manhood in the agony of death when the godhead left him, who cried out my God, my God, why haft thou forfaken me!—Can there be a greater evidence that God was in Christ, than the man Christ praying to him?—who did not return to him again till he raifed him in his glorious body, and fet him on his right hand, to be King of Kings, Lord of Lords, and Judge of the world.

On Nicodemus coming to *Jefus* for inftruction he anfwered and faid, *verily, verily I fay unto thee, except a man be born again, he cannot fee the kingdom of God.* On Nicodemus's unbelief, *Jefus* anfwered, *verily, verily I fay unto thee, except a man be born of water, and of the fpirit, he cannot enter the kingdom of God.*—Thefe are *the words of Jefus Chrift*—and Mr. *Porter* agrees † " that it is *impious* to doubt, that all which was faid " by Chrift, was faid by God."—Thus it may be obferved, *that if we are not born again, we cannot fee the kingdom of God:* but this new birth muft be in this life; and St. John tells us how we are to attain it ‡ That *as many as received him* (Chrift) *to them he gave power to become the fons of God,* even *to them that believe in his name, which were born* not of blood, *nor of the will of the flefh, nor of the will of man,* but of God, as St. Paul tells us,‖ *ye are all* the *children of God* by faith in Chrift Jefus, and St. John alfo fay;, that

B   *who-*

* Phil. iii. 21. † P. 5. Letter to Dr. H. ‡ John i. 12, 13. ‖ Gal, iii. 26.

whofoever believed that *Jefus* is *Chrift,* is born *of God;*§
and that *he that believeth on the Son hath eternal life,*†
and he that *believeth* not *the Son fhall* not *fee life, but the
wrath of God abideth in him* * And Jefus told his Dif-
ciples, after his refurrection,‡ *he that believeth and is
baptized fhall be faved;* but he *that believeth not fhall be
damned* **

By the above paffages in fcripture we may obferve how we muft be born again to inherit a new
and eternal life, and a refurrection after death—
that is, by a *true faith in Chrift.*—How dreadful is
unbelief! but how comfortable is it to him that believeth on the Son, who, St. John tells us, has
everlafting life, and fhall arife again to a glorious
and eternal life, which, that we may all do, let us
ufe the words of the Pfalmift†† in prayer to *Jehovah, that he will open our eyes* that we *may behold the
wonderous things out of his law;* and that he will cleanfe
the thoughts of our hearts, and give us power to
overcome our prejudices; by the infpiration of his
holy fpirit.

CHAP.

§ 1 John v. 1 † John iii. 15. * John iii. 26. ‡ Mark xvi. 16.

** This may be thought a harfh faying by many in this *humane* age,
who think their own *reafon* (which is their *idol)* fuperior to the word
of God —But let us agree with Mr. *Porter,* and believe it, as it was
faid by Chrift himfelf after his refurrection , for, fays Mr. P. ‖ "it is
"*impious to doubt,* that *all* which was faid by Jefus Chrift was faid
" by God."

†† Pf. cxix. 18.

‖ *Letter to Dr.* H p 5

C H A P. II.

On the Scriptures of the Old Teſlament.

HAVING done with Mr. *Porter* on the New Teſtament, I ſhall now make ſome obſervations on what he ſays on the *Hebrew text* of the Old Teſtament, which were the ſcriptures that Chriſt bids the Jews to ſearch—for, ſays he, they are which teſtify of me. * However, for Mr. *Porter*'s Amuſement, I will give him a text or two more, for him to exerciſe his *ingenuity* on, viz. 2 Cor. v. 19. GOD was in Chriſt, who hath reconciled the world to HIMSELF.—Rom. ix. 5. St. Paul ſays, (ſpeaking of the Iſraelites) of whom as concerning the fleſh CHRIST *came,* who is over all, GOD bleſſed for ever.—Does not this text inform us that *Chriſt was both God and man ?*—St. Paul tells the Elders of the church Acts xx. 28. to *feed the church of GOD which he hath* purchaſed with his OWN BLOOD.—1 John iii. 16. *Hereby perceive we the love* of GOD, becauſe he has laid down HIS LIFE for us.—1 John v. 20. *We are in him* that is true, even in his SON JESUS CHRIST. *This is the* TRUE GOD and eternal Life.

Mr. *Porter* criticiſes on the *Hebrew Scriptures,* which were revelations from Jehovah himſelf, with as much freedom, as if he underſtood them ever ſo

B 2   well,

* John v. 39.

well, though it does not appear that he knows one letter from another of the *Hebrew alphabet*; but all this is done by his own *intuitive* and *infallible* REASON.—See with what authority he does it!

"There is not (says he) a *single text* to be found "in the Old Testament, which favours the doctrine "of a *plurality* of perfons in the Divine Effence;— "the confequence of which is, that the Jews always "have been, and ftill continue to be ftrenuous ad- "vocates of the Divine Unity.†—The pronouns "ufed with refpect to this ONE GOD, are all fin- "gular. *I, thou, he, thee, him.*"

It might be imagined, that by thefe *confident* and *dogmatical* affertions, Mr. *Porter* had examined the *original Hebrew* of the Old Teftament, as well as the Englifh tranflation, before he had afferted fo much, but it does not appear that he is capable of examining the original, neither does it appear that he had paid much attention to the Englifh Bible; for, had he done it, he might obferve that Gen. 1. 26. "And " God faid, let US make man in OUR own image, " after OUR own likenefs."—Gen. III. 22. "And " the LORD GOD faid, behold the man is become " as one of US."*

I fhall

† Mi P. p. 9, 10.

* It may be obferved that the Hebrew words for *Lord God* are אלהים יהוה IeHOVaH ALEIM, or as it is generally founded *Elohim* — *Jehovah* is a fingular without a plural, and never applied to any but the felf-exifting eternal Effence.—*Elohim* is and muft be

I fhall only add two more texts, that is Gen. xi.
6, 7. " And the LORD *(Jehovah)* faid—let US go
" down, &c." and Ifa. vi. 8. " And I heard the
" voice of the Lord, faying—who will go for US."

The above quotations are from the Englifh Bible,
where the pronouns joined to *Jehovah* are plural,
which, Mr. *Porter,* ought to have obferved, had he
examined his bible, as a critic ought to do, *before he
fo confidently afferts* that " ALL the pronouns ufed to
" this ONE GOD are fingular."—But I have the
charity to hope that he did not make the above affertions, knowing them to be falfe, but that he had
never examined the fcriptures with proper attention.
If he will confult any one who underftands them in
the original, he will alfo find a number of places befides where God is joined with *plural nouns, pronouns,
verbs, and adjectives* , as, perhaps, he may doubt it,
I will

---

plural, fignifying as an attribute a title of office, as *federators, covenanters,* or any bound by oath to perform an office, hence applied to
princes, kings, governors, &c. in like manner as בראיך BoRAICH
does, Eccles. xii. 1. where this Hebrew word is plural, and the tranflation of the Hebrew is, " remember thy CREATORS," in the plural, *not Creator,* in the fingular, as in our Englifh Bible.——The
Jews and all others who underftand the Hebrew do and muft agree
that the Lord God is mentioned here as in confultation.—I think
there does not appear to be a text in the Hebrew Bible more expreffive
of a plurality in the felf-exifting Effence than this. In the firft part
of the verfe the *Lord God* is joined to a verb fingular, and at the latter
part of the verfe expreffes *himfelf* or *themfelves* in the plural like one
of US.—See p. 16.

I will point out a few, viz. Gen. xx. 13.—xxxv. 7.
2 Sam. vii. 23.—Deut. ix. 7.—Joſhua xxiv. 19.—
Pſalm lviii. 12. &c.

In Gen. xxxv. 7. we read, " that he *(Jacob)* built
" an altar and called the place אל בית אל EL BETH
"EL," that is, a houſe or building to EL, *(God)*
becauſe (האלהים *He Elohim* the demonſtrative *He* be
ing prefixed to ſhew that they were the *true Elohim,*
God, his *Covenanters,* his *Creators, as it is in the Hebrew)* THEN appeared unto him. We may under-
ſtand from this verſe that the *Elohim,* his *Creators,*
the *Trinity,* appeared unto him, but that he built
there, according to their command, an altar to אל
EL the *Logos,* who was to take manhood, and become the *Meſſiah,* to *expreſs his faith* that he would
become his Redeemer as God had promiſed. +

This EL was the ſame *name* of God as the man
Chriſt called on in the agony of death on the croſs,
where he cried אלי אלי למה שבקתני ELI, ELI, LaMaH Sa-
BaT HoNI, * only with an additional *jod* or pronoun

my,

+ Moſes in this chapter tells us that *Iſaac* now repeated the pro-
phetic bleſſing he had before given to *Jacob,* and that the *Elohim*
appeared unto him and confirmed the promiſe to *his* feed, which he
had before made to *Abraham* and to *Iſaac,* and bleſſed him, therefore, according to God's command, by faith in his promiſe, and as a
memorial of it, he built there an altar, and called it בית אל BETH EL,
in Engliſh a *houſe* or building to EL, GOD. For, ſays he, thus is
none other but the houſe of God.

* Pſ. xxii. 1. and Matth. xxvii. 46.

y, and in the fingular number.—This is the fame
perfon of the Effence, by the fame name which
Ifaiah ‡ prophefied fhould be incarnate in the womb
of *the Virgin.*—" Therefore, (fays Ifaiah) the Lord
" himfelf fhall give you *a fign*, (behold *the fign!)*
" THE VIRGIN fhall conceive and bear a fon, and
" fhall call his name *Immanuel*, אל EL, GOD *with us.*"

This EL is the fame perfon of the Effence, by the
fame name, who *Ifaiah* alfo prophefied fhould take
upon him the manhood.—" For, fays he, unto us a
" child is born, unto us a fon is given, and the go-
" vernment fhall be upon his fhoulder ; and his name
" fhall be called Wonderful, Counfeller, the mighty
" God, the everlafting FATHER, the Prince of
" Peace." §

Mr. *Porter* by his *intuitive* knowledge in the Hebrew fcriptures tells us, " that mighty God, *fhould*
" *more properly be* a mighty God, 'a name (fays he)
" which may furely be applied to Jefus Chrift with
" as much propriety as it was to *Mofes, Kings, Angels*
" and *Magiftrates.*"—Here Mr. *Porter* would appear
to be an able and *learned critic* on the *Hebrew fcriptures;* but I could wifh that he would endeavour to
get a better knowledge of them before he makes thefe
affertions.—I will endeavour to explain the caufe
of his miftake !—There are many different words in
Hebrew fcriptures, which in the Englifh Bible is tranflated

‡ Ifaiah vii. 14.   § Ifaiah ix. 6.

lated by the general name God, which gives a *par-ticular attribute* to him, that is not taken notice of in the tranflation.—Thus אלהים *Elohim* is the noun that *Jehovah* firft made ufe of to exprefs himfelf to man and is moft commonly made ufe of in the fcripture for God, and has been obferved * already to be the firft name that the eternal Effence revealed himfelf to man. It is a noun plural, exprefſive of office concerning the creation and redemption; derived as lexicons point out to us, from אלה ALaH an oath

In *Avenarius's* lexicon, which was printed more than two hundred years ago, you have the follow-ing explanation of it under אלה ALOE.—*Deus—tribuitur quoque diis ficticiis item angelis hominibus quando* loco Dei *funt in judicio*—et *in plural* Gen. i. 1. אלהים Elohim *in principio creavit* Dii *cælum* & *terram*—i—TRINITAS creavit.

Thus it may be obferved that this is the comfort-able name that *Jehovah* revealed himfelf or *themfelves* to man, having before the creation covenanted by oath amongft themfelves, concerning his redempti-on, in cafe he fell, which St. Paul tells us † *was the wifdom of God* in a myftery, *even a* hidden *wifdom, which God ordained* before *the world unto our glory: In hope of* everlafting life, *which God that cannot lie pro-mifed* before *the world began* ; ‡ *who hath faved us, and called us with an holy calling, not according to our works, but according to his own purpofe and grace, which was*
given

* See note to p. 12.　　† 1 Cor. ii. 7.　　‡ Tit. i. 2.

given us in Chrift Jefus before the world began, *
who was the lamb flain *from the foundation of the*
world. ‡

This word *Elohim* as *Avenarius* informs us, in a
derivative fenfe is applied to Mofes, to Angels,
Kings, and Magiftrates, when they fat in judgement
in the place of God. †

Had Mr. *Porter* been able to read the Hebrew
fcriptures, he would have found, that in this text
of *Ifaiah*, the word which is tranflated God, is not
אלהים *Elohim*, but אל EL, with גבור GeBOR added
to it, fignifying the *ftrong*, the *mighty*, fo that it muft
be the ftrong, the mighty EL *God* —אל EL fignifies
the *ftrong God*, the *Logos*, and is not applied either
to Mofes, to Kings, or Magiftrates.—It is applied
to the fecond perfon in the Effence ! And here to
make it the more clear אל EL is joined to גבור Ge-
BOR, a participle paffive, from גבר GeBaR, fignifying to be ftrong, mighty, to prevail, who *was* to prevail ; and applied particularly to the King of Glory
(Chrift) who *was* to prevail as the Pfalmift informs
us. ‖ Who is the King of Glory ? " *Jehovah*, the
" Lord, ftrong and mighty ;" and applied by St.
Paul to Chrift, § " that every tongue fhould confefs
" that Jefus Chrift is Lord, to the glory of God the
" Father."

C

Thus

---

* 2 Tim. i. ix.　　‡ Rev. xiii. 8.　　† See note to p. 12.
‖ Pf. xxiv. 8.　　§ Phil. ii. 11.

Thus Mr. *Porter* by his confident affertions and criticifms has with, *much appearance of erudition,* expofed his ignorance of the original.—Then follows the common affertion of a corruption, for (fays he) " it is *highly probable* the original text is corrupted, " for the Vatican copy of the Septuagint wants the " expreffion Wonderful, Counfeller, mighty God." Thus having found one copy of a *tranflation* from the Hebrew *deficient*, where the words he diflikes moft are not to be found ; (whether the deficiency is wanting either wilfully or not) he takes upon him to fay, *as ufual*, with a text he does not like, that *there is a corruption in the original,* and *all other copies.* As this is fo expreffive of the divinity and power of Chrift, I do not wonder he fhould fo much defire to get rid of it !

He then goes on to affert, " that throughout the " whole of the Old Teftament, but ONE being is " mentioned, the creator and preferver of the world; " this Being (fays he) is uniformly fpoken of as *one* " *perfon,* and is faid to have made the world imme- " diately by himfelf, thus Gen. i. 1. In the begin- " ning," &c. *

Mr. *Porter* here feems to have chofen a text to exprefs the *Unity* of the Godhead, which, had he underflood in the original Hebrew, he would have found, as has been already obferved, that it exprefs- ed quite the contrary.† The word *Elohim* God is

and

* See note to p. 5, 6, 7.   † Note 5, p. 7.

and muſt be plural, and in Eccleſiaſtes‡ they are called *Creators* in the plural, *not* Creator in the ſingular. Thus in the Hebrew bible it is there ſaid—" remember thy Creators in the days of thy youth;" not Creator in the ſingular, as it is tranſlated in our Engliſh bible.

It is remarkable that *Jehovah* makes uſe of this name *Elohim* for God, throughout the whole hiſtory of the creation, and repeats it in every verſe, till the creation is finiſhed, when cap. ii. 3. *Elohim* God is ſaid to have finiſhed it and to have reſted the ſeventh day, and bleſſed the ſeventh day and ſanctified it, *becauſe* in it he reſted from all his work. In the next verſe we are told that *Jehovah Elohim* the Lord God made the earth and the heavens.—*Jehovah* here joined to *Elohim* (God) appears to point out to us the *plurality* in the *Godhead*, and the *unity* of *Jehovah*, the *ſelf-exiſting Eſſence!* and informs us who theſe *Covenanters* or *Creators* to perform the Creation and Redemption were, the *eternal and ſelf-exiſting* Jehovah! and not created Angels, as ſome Jews, as well as ſome who call themſelves Chriſtians, have imagined, and that *Jehovah Elohim* the Lord our God (our Creators) were ONE Jehovah, ONE ſelf-exiſtent Being.

Mr. *Porter* after treating the ſcriptures concerning the Divinity of Chriſt as above, by *ſuppoſing corruptions, interpolations,* &c. now goes farther, and at-

tributes

‡ Ecclef. xii. 1.

tributes an *untruth* to them, and produces a text, though nothing to the purpose he was treating about; but, that if it was untrue it might leſſen the authority of the ſcriptures, and thereby theſe texts of ſcriptures which pertained to the divinity of Chriſt. Thus he tells us that Joſhua x. 12, 13. " Sun ſtand thou ſtill." &c. *has been demonſtrated to be falſe.*—Had he been a Critic in the Hebrew language he would have found that the word שמש SHe-MoSH, which is there tranſlated *Sun*, as well as in other parts of the Engliſh bible, never throughout the *Hebrew* bible ſignifies the body of the ſun, but the *ſolar light* proceeding from it. Whenever the *body* of the ſun is mentioned in the Hebrew bible it is called חמה CHaMaH, and the body of the moon לבנה LiBNaH, as may be obſerved Iſaiah xxx. 26. " The light of the *moon* ſhall be as the light of the " ſun, and the light of the ſun ſhall be ſeven-fold." Thus alſo, as is obſerved, in our Engliſh tranſlation, the *ſun* is ſaid to riſe and ſet; but it is not found ſo in the original, where the morning is deſcribed by the *ſhemoſh* or ſolar light *ſpringing out,* and the evening darkneſs by the ſolar light *going in,* or hid by the darkneſs. Can the beſt Naturaliſt give a more clear or expreſſive deſcription of evening and morning than this in the original! where the morning is deſcribed by the *ſolar light* ſpringing forth, and the evening by the ſolar light going in and covered with darkneſs.

Dr.

Dr. *Horne*, the late Bishop of Norwich, in his celebrated Paraphrase on the Psalms, points out to us the 19th Psalm as descriptive of the *rule, law,* or *powers* of Nature :—Thus in this Psalm we are told that " the *heavens declare* or *shew forth the glory of God,* and the firmament *(which is expanded from the sun to the extremities of the system)* his handy work, their line or (as it is in the margin of the Bible) their *rule* or direction is gone out through the whole earth; in them he hath placed a tabernacle to the sun (Hebrew *the solar light)* which is as a bridegroom coming out of his chamber, and rejoiceth as a strong man to run a race, his CIRCUIT (or circulation) to the ends of it. (Hebrew *them)* and there is nothing hid from the heat thereof. Heb. *them.)* *

Thus

* Here the Psalmist informs us that the *heavens* shew us the glory of God, and the firmament shew us his handy work, or the strength of his hands. The Hebrew word made use of to denote the *heavens* is שמים SHeMIM. Lexicographers agree that this word is the plural masculine (as is *Elohim)* of שם SHeM, a name given to persons or things, to *give us an idea and explain the thing named*; and it is observable that *Shemim* the plural masculine of *Shem* is not applied to any thing but to the *heavens*; the plural for names given to persons or things is feminine שמות SHeMOTH. Hence many of the learned have thought by this psalm and other places in scripture, that the heavens were pointed out to us (as this psalm expresses) as emblems, or representations of the *Trinity in Unity*, as the words *Jehovah Elohim* does in Gen. ii. 5 § ——The expansion of the heavens being of *one substance* with *three distinct* powers or qualities, composed of *fire* at the body of the sun, *light* proceeding from it, and *cold* or *spirit* returning from the extremities to it. The Psalmist also tells us, that

§ See p. 19.

Thus we are here told in *Joshua* that the SHe. MoSH the *solar light* was *silent still* and did not go off, but remained on *Gibeon*, and יַרֵח JaReCH the reflected light from the moon in the valley of *Ajalon*. Hence it may be obferved in this miracle that neither the *sun,* the *moon,* or earth are mentioned, or the motion of either of them concerned about it.— Can it be imagined that either the body of the fun was on Gibeon, or the body of the moon in the valley of Ajalon?—It was only (as the *Hebrew expreffes* it) the *solar light* and the *lunar light* remained in both thefe places, till *Joshua* had deftroyed his enemies! The *solar light* and the *lunar light* remained in both places in a fupernatural manner (contrary to the law of Nature!) The length of time that this fupernatural light remained there, was *one whole day;* or while the earth made one revolution on its axis.

As thefe three qualities, powers, or laws of nature, are in continual circulation, going out in light from the body of the *fun* to the extremities of the fyftem, and returning to the fun *again,* in the quality of *cold* or *fpirit,* there to be melted down and fent out again as before. *Job†* in defcribing thefe *agents, laws,* or *powers of Nature,* fays, " Has thou expanded out the fky *(firmament)* which ftrong as a molten " looking-glafs (Hebrew, like the fufion of a *fpeculum,* which requires " the *greateft heat* to diffolve it)"——שְׁחָקִים SHeCHeKIM, tranflated *fky,* fignifies the atoms of the heavens in continual conflict, (the firft agent in nature) which are continually forced out from the fun, expanded throughout all nature, and returning again from the extremities of the fyftem, which by their *conflict, forces* every thing in clofer contact, and binds all matter together. This word *Shechekim* fky, Pf, lxxxix. 6. fignifies heaven, and is fo tranflated.

† Job xxxvii. 18.

As this miracle was performed by the Lord *(Je-hovah)* caufing the light from the fun and the light from the moon to remain *ſtill* or in one place for one day, or while the earth made one revolution on its axis, fo *Jehovah* caufed a darknefs over the land of Egypt * three days, or whilft the earth made three revolutions round its axis.

Thus we find that SHeMoSH, the *folar light*, and JaReCH, the *lunar light*, remained *ſtill*, without motion, in both thefe places, in a miraculous manner, contrary to the laws or mechanifm of nature—But that חמה CHaMaH or the body of the fun, and לבנה LiBNaH the body of the moon, were at the fame time in their places in the heavens, doing the offices appointed to them, and the earth continued her ufual motions. It does not appear that any difference in light or darknefs was occafioned on any other parts of the earth but only on *Gibeon*, and in the valley of *Ajalon* !

I leave thefe remarks with the reader, without fubjoining any obfervations, that he may form his own conclufions of the juftice with which Mr. *Porter* hath charged fcripture of an *untruth* in the cafe of Jofhua.

CHAP.

* Exod. x. 21, 22, 23.

C H A P. III.

On Mr. Porter's second Reply to Dr. Hawker.

THE Remarks in the preceding chapters were made on reading the controverfy between Dr. Hawker and Mr. *Porter*, and put *by* without a defign of publifhing, till Mr. *Porter* publifhed his reply to Dr. *Hawker*; in which he *domineers* and tells him that he paffed over *Jofhua* x. 12. in a *vague* manner, † and ftill continued to affert that the fcriptures related facts *contrary* to what was truth.—On reading thofe bold affertions, I thought it my duty, (as a believer in Chrift, and having faith in the fcriptures) to vindicate them: On this belief, I have offered thefe remarks to the public; if they convince any one of their errors in faith, or ftrengthen others that are wavering or unfettled, I fhall think myfelf happy to have done it.

With refpect to the controverfy between Dr. *Hawker* and Mr. *Porter* I have nothing to do.—It is in defence of the fcriptures in their original language that I feel concerned, and I hope I have fairly and fully fhewn Mr. *Porter's* incompetency in the argument.

I cannot at the fame time help obferving that Mr. *Porter* would have done no injury to his caufe had he ufed a different kind of language in the beginning of his reply to Dr. *Hawker*, and inftead of

making

† P. 34.

making ufe of fuch vulgar and difingenuous, (which is not very genteel, neither is it pleafant to read) it would have been kind to point out thefe *blunders*;—for *reafoning genteely* is much more convincing than calling names—but Mr. *Porter* appears to be nettled with Dr. *Hawker*, and fays, " his infinuation that there is an intimate connection between *Unitarianifm* and *Deifm* is *illiberal* and *ill-founded*: It appears to me (fays Mr. *Porter)* that he could have made it with no other view, than that of placing *Unitarianifm* in the worft light."†—

I was much pleafed to obferve that he was angry by comparing *Unitarianifm* to *Deifm* It looks as if he had fome veneration for the fcriptures !—By this and fome other parts of his reply, which will be taken notice of hereafter, there appears a hope that his intention is *fincere*, and that he may be *convinced* of his erroneous opinions ; (for he fays) " that *Unitarianifm* having an intimate connection with *Deifm* is placing it in the *worft light poffible !'* —By this obfervation of his, I fhould imagine he puts a different meaning on the word *Deifm*, than it is generally taken in.—I fhall therefore give Dr. *Johnfon's* definition of the meaning of the word !—He tells us " that *Deifm* is derived from the French *Deifme*—the " opinion of thofe who acknowledge *one God*, with- " out the reception of *any* revealed religion."

Mr. *Porter* defcribes a *Unitarian* to be a perfon

D   who

who acknowledges *one God*; and allows to be true such parts of the scriptures, as *suits* his REASON and *what will answer his purpose*, and denies the rest. Thus, as Christ was both God and man, some part of which speak of his Godhead, whilst other part relate to his manhood, Mr. *Porter* brings these part to oppose each other, hoping thereby to prove their inconsistency; and with regard to their genuine ness, in his Defence of Unitarianism, he objects to many texts; but in his Reply, he gets rid of them by wholesale, and tells us of a friend of his who asserts, that there are *six hundred futile reading*, in the Greek of the New Testament.*—With regard to the Hebrew scriptures of the Old Testament, which our Saviour *bids the Jews to search*, he tells us that those parts which do not suit his REASON, are *interpolated, corrupted*, or *speak untruths*. Hence he appears a more subtle adversary against God and his revelation, than a *Deist* who denies them in the whole; therefore he cannot make use of one part against another, as Mr. *Porter* has done.

In this manner did the old serpent beguile Eve! He did not deny that there was a God, or that God had made a revelation to man, but he persuaded her to trust to her *own senses* and REASON, and told her that some parts of it was *false*, as her own *senses and reason* told her.—Thus, he acted the part neither of an *Atheist*, nor did he act the part of a *Deist*, denying

ying that God had made a revelation to man; but
s a *subtle deceiver*, making ufe of what part of reve-
ation fuited him, and putting an infidious meaning
on the reft, perfuading her to truft to her own fenfes
and reafon, and not to what God had revealed.—
Yea (fays he) *hath God faid ye fhall not eat, left ye
die.—Ye fhall not furely die, for God doth know, that
in the day ye eat thereof, then your eyes fhall be
opened. And when the woman faw that it was good
for food, and that it was pleafant to the eyes, and a tree
to be defired to make one wife, fhe took of the fruit thereof
and did eat.* Hence it may be obferved, *that the deceiver* from the beginning did not deny the revelation
of God, but made ufe of *more fubtle means*, denying
fome part, and putting a wrong conftruction on the
reft.—Mr. *Porter* will be able to judge whether any
part of the above hiftory may be applied to the
Unitarian!

The fcriptures inform us that want of *faith* in the
revelation of God was the caufe of the fall of Eve
and Adam, which was brought on and encouraged by
the enticement of the old ferpent : Our unbelief in
the word of God has been continued ever fince, by
the fuggeftions of the evil fpirit.—Thus faid he to
Eve, ye fhall not furely die, and reafoned with her
about the fine appearance and goodnefs of the fruit,
which, as it appeared good to the eye, fhe thought
her fenfes could not deceive her. Thus believing
the inftigations of the evil fpirit, and trufting to her

own

own fenfes and reafon, fhe brought death on herfelf
and all her pofterity—however, on the repentance
of Adam and her, and a faith in the promifed Meffiah, they were forgiven.—Some fuppofe in allufion
to this, that the animals flain, were emblematical
of his death, fo were the coats of fkins, with which
God covered their bodies, emblematical of his merits
covering their fin—Then he gave them the promife
of him, that he fhould bruife the ferpent's head, and
that his heel fhould be bruifed by the ferpent ; and
notwithftanding their prefent bodies were to be deftroyed by death, yet by *faith in the Meffiah*, and his
fufferings and refurrection, they fhould be raifed
again to a *new life*, with a *new and glorious body*.

Now it may be obferved that want of faith in the
word of God and of Chrift, and trufting to our own
fenfes and reafon ; in oppofition to it, have been the
caufe of all unrighteoufnefs ; therefore, in order to
know the difference between *Reafon* and *Faith*, let
us examine how each of them are attained.

Reafon is gained by the ideas we receive by our
bodily fenfes, and what we learn by converfation,
reading, &c.—*We have none innate!*—As all our ideas
are received by our fenfes, fo, a man deftitute of one
of his fenfes can never have an idea belonging to
that fenfe, and fuppofing him to be deftitute of *all*
fenfes, he would have *no idea* at all.—Hence we may
obferve, that our reafon is formed by the ideas we
receive by our *bodily fenfes, converfation,* and *reading,*

and

and that it is *not innate* but acquired. The mind or animal foul comes into the world a *charte blanche*, and is that principle whereby comparing the feveral ideas we receive by our fenfes, we have a power to combine, unite, and feparate thofe ideas; and it is found by the experience of all, that the ideas firft imprinted thereon, either by our fenfes or converfation, reading, or what we are taught, make fuch deep impreffions on it, that it is with the greateft difficulty that they can be eradicated, let them be ever fo faulty.

Thus a perfon inftructed in the doctrine of the Church of England, which is derived from the fcriptures, will believe in a Trinity; a plurality in the divine Effence; the Divinity of Chrift, &c.—whilft thofe on the contrary, who are inftructed by the interpretation put on them by the Socinians and Unitarians, will deny both. We may carry this farther! Many of the ancients believed the fun to be God, and worfhipped him as fuch.—And the Atheifts (though it is *almoft* contrary to reafon, to believe there is a poffibility to be fuch, had it not been acknowledged lately in the National Affembly of France!) who believe no God.—Many, after they have acquired ideas in this manner, *think them innate,* and will argue that they are *innate,* and proper to *direct* them in what is *right* and *wrong,* and think themfelves right *fincere* in doing it, and tell us that they have reafon on their fide; but the fcriptures

infoim

inform us " *that the heart of the sons of men is full of*
" *evil;* * *for whatsoever is not of faith is sin.*" ‡

Hence it may be observed, that our reason will
carry us *from life to death,* but no farther.—It may do
for an Atheist !—but gives no information or notion
of God or a future state: Indeed, the emblem which
Christ pointed to us by *the grain of wheat dying in the
ground, and then bringing forth much fruit,* † gives us
some notion that God may raise us again after death
and corruption to a new life ; for the grain after
rotting, and again becoming *ground,* from whence it
was, is by the power of the natural agents, *light* or
heat, and *water*, made to spring again to a beautiful
plant ; even so the souls of the faithful will be *raised
again by the spiritual light and the holy spirit.*

Our reason may carry us from the beginning of
life to death, but we can have no idea from our
senses and reason that we are to be raised again, this
must be done by *faith* in Jesus Christ, and the gift
of grace, which is attained by hearing, reading, and
believing the scriptures, which inform us that
grace is the gift of God, given to those who
believe.

It having been shown that we can know nothing
of our creation and futurity but what God hath revealed, let us apply to his revelation, which tells us
that our first parents transgressed against the word
of God, by which they were condemned to die,

(which

---

* Ecclef. ix. 3.   ‡ Rom. xiv. 23.   † John xii. 24.

(which *reafon tells us we muft all undergo,* as we fee it
fpares none) but on their repentance, he told them
that the *feed of the woman* fhould bruife the ferpent's
head, which certainly implied the doctrine of a
Meffiah, a Saviour, who fhould be without fin, and
undergo the curfe pronounced on man, and by his
refurrection reftore him to a *new* and glorious life;
and that the terms of acceptance was a true *faith*
in him: Now *faith* is in oppofition to reafon, one
is of the flefh *earthly,* whilft the other is *fpiritually*
from heaven—*Reafon inftructs us in earthly things,
Faith in heavenly!*

The fcriptures inform us that *Faith is the fubftance
of things hoped for, the evidence of things not feen;* *
*that through Faith we underftand that the worlds were
framed by the word of God.* * That *this Faith is obtained by reading and hearing the fcriptures read;* † *fo
Faith is obtained by reading and hearing the fcriptures
with humility, with a defire of fcriptural affiftance to underftand them.* ‡ *Faith is the gift of God*; for *by grace
are ye faved through Faith, and not of yourfelves, left
any man fhould boaft* § *that we muft be born again through
Faith in the Meffiah Chrift our Saviour,* who was to be
God and man, as Ifaiah prophefied of him; ‖ *I, even
I am* JEHOVAH, *and* befides me *there is* no SAVI-
OUR.—Ifaiah alfo prophefied that the fign the
Lord would give was to be, *that* a virgin *fhould conceive*

---

* Heb. xi. 1, 3.　　† Rom. x. 17.　　‡ Pf. cxix. 18.
§ Eph. ii. 8.　　‖ Ifa. xliii. 11.

ceive and bear a fon, and they fhall call his name† Immanuel, which by tranflation is God with us. St. *Paul* tells us *he was the Lord from heaven* ;* and Ifaiah farther informs us,‡ that this child born fhould be *the mighty God, the everlafting Father, the Prince of Peace* ; *who died for our fins,*|| *being juftified freely by his grace* ; *through the redemption that is in Jefus Chrift, to be* a propitiation *through* Faith *in his blood* ; *to declare his righteoufnefs for the remiffion of fins that are paft* ;§ *for the juft fhall live by Faith* ;** thus as he told *Nicodemus*, we muft be born again to inherit the kingdom of God ; *that being juftified by his grace, we fhall be made heirs according to the hope of eternal life* ;§§ that is, we muft have a true faith to believe that he has undergone the death denounced on Adam and all his pofterity, that he has *endured the curfe* for us ; *as in Adam all die, even fo in Chrift fhall all be made alive* ;†† *the firft man is of the earth earthy, the fecond man is the Lord from heaven* ; by Faith in *whofe blood we fhall inherit* a new *life, and be juftified by a belief in Jefus Chrift* ;‡‡ *for ye are all the children of God by Faith in Jefus Chrift* ,|||| *for as many as received him* to them gave *he power to become the fons of God, even to them that believe in his name* ;*** for as our Saviour tells us, *we muft be born of water and of the fpirit* ; and St. Paul, *that if thou fhall confefs with thy mouth the Lord Jefus,*

---

† Ifa. vii. 14.　* 1 Cor. xv. 47.　‡ Ifa. ix. 6.　|| Rom. iii. 24.
§ Rom. iii. 25.　** Rom. i. 17.　§§ Tit. iii. 7.　†† 1 Cor.
xv. 22.　‡‡ Rom, iii. 26.　|||| Gal. iii. 26.　*** John i, 12.

Jefus, and fhalt believe in thine heart that God hath raifed him from the dead, thou fhalt be faved. *—Thus Jefus preaching to the Jews told them,† *your father Abra- ham rejoiced to fee my day, and he faw it and was glad;* which the Jews difbelieving, he anfwered them, *verily, verily, before Abraham was* I AM.—The Jews remembering that I AM; was the name that God told *Mofes* he fhould make him known by to the children of Ifrael;‡ they believed he talked blafphe- my, and took up ftones to caft at him, as it was the command of their law to ftone thofe that blafphemed. Jefus faid unto them, *if ye believe not that* I AM, *ye fhall die in your fins*; and, St. Peter, when he was ex- amined before the High Prieft and Caiaphas, told them, *that there was none other name under heaven given among men whereby we may be faved, but the name of Jefus Chrift:* || And this is confirmed by other fcrip- tures, *For he that believeth on him, is not condemned; but he that believeth not is condemned already, becaufe he hath not believed in the only begotten Son of God. For he that believeth on the Son hath everlafting life: and he that believeth not the Son, fhall not fee life,* §— This is confirmed by Jefus himfelf after his refur- rection, who told his Apoftles when he fent them forth to preach the gofpel—*He that believeth,* (faith Chrift) *and is baptized, fhall be faved, but he that be- lieveth not fhall be damned.* **

E

What

---

* Rom. x. 9, † John viii. 56, 58, ‡ Exod. iii. 14,
|| Acts iv. 12, § John iii. 18, 36, ** Mark xvi. 16,

What hath been obferved concerning Reafon, fhews us how inadequate it is to direct us in the me-thod of falvation, though Mr. *Porter* tells us, " that " however widely he may differ, provided we are " equally *fincere*, we fhall hereafter meet and agree " together in the prefence of our common God and " Father." So that a *Turk*, a *Heathen of any kind*, let his idolatry be what it may, fo that he is *fincere* in his belief, will meet together with the believer in Chrift, and agree at the laft day!—But the fcriptures inform us the contrary, and affure us, that there is no falvation but by Faith in Chrift, which will make us heirs of a refurrection after death to a new and glorious life. If this be the cafe, how careful ought we to be that we have a true Faith in him! There-fore as it has been fhewn, how eafy our reafon is corrupted, and as Chriftians agree that hearing and reading the fcriptures are the method to attain knowledge to falvation ; and, as our Saviour told the Jews, it was for want of believing them that they did not believe him ; let us read them (if we can) in the original, without *paraphrafe* or *comment*, with humility, and a defire of inftruction—let us compare fcripture with fcripture ; one text will ex-plain another :—If fome parts appear difficult and obfcure, they will be explained by others.—If we meet with *myfteries* which we cannot underftand, as the *incarnation, refurrection*, &c. let us believe them, as they are revealed to us from God ; though, whilft

we

we are flesh and blood, we cannot *comprehend* them, as they are *spiritual*;—let us not disbelieve them because Mr. *Porter* has pointed out a different reading in a translation from the original.—And, as reading sceptical authors misguides our reason, let us abstain from such authors as Dr. *Middleton, Sykes, Lindsey, Priestley,* &c. together with *Westein* ; and *Griesbach* ; who is Mr. *Porter*'s oracle, and who tell us in a long quotation from him, where, he says, " I could, in-" deed, if it were of consequence, defend *six hundred* " of the most futile readings" *(of the New Testament)* ' " nay, says he, more in number."*—These authors I am fearful are such as the Psalmist describes—*They wrest my words;—all their thoughts are against me for evil.*‖

To point out what reliance we ought to put in such authors, I shall only mention one instance, and that from his favourite *Griesbach,* to whom he tells Dr. *Hawker* he always refers.—But, says Mr. *Porter* to Dr. *Hawker,* " I suppose you read books with-" out taking the trouble to refer to the notes ; or " perhaps you never before heard of the names " of *Westein* or *Griesbach.*"—This is one of the many flowers of controversy that the learned Mr. *Porter* makes use of! by which, together with his *long tran-scripts* from his Socinian and Unitarian authors, he finds but little trouble to compose his letter—for in one place he has a transcript from his *learned Gries-bach,* which fills more than three pages,† to prove

E 3   that

---

* Letter to Dr. H. p. 17.   ‖ Ps. lvi. 5.   † Letter to Dr. H. p. 28.

that 1 John, v. 7. is an interpolation, who says,
" that in many Latin manuscripts it is also wanting.
" The first who clearly cites this suspected text is
" *Vigilius Tapsensis*, about the end of the 5th century;
" and it chiefly, or *rather entirely depends* upon his
" credit and authority; but he was an obscure au-
" thor."—The contrary of this will be found to be
true; and to prove it so, I think it unnecessary to
produce any other evidence than that of *Tertullian*,
who was cotemporary with *Polycarp*,—and *Polycarp*
is supposed to be ordained bishop by St. John, who
used to take delight in relating the discourses he had
with him.—*Tertullian* in defending the Trinity a-
gainst *Praxeas*, (who acknowledged but One person
in God, making no distinction between the Father
and Son) he *(Tertullian)* tells him the rule of Faith,
" which acknowledges one God in three Persons,
" which are all of the same substance, and have *all*
" the same power, and that it was the person of the
" Son who was incarnate.—The following are his
" words, *Connexus patris in filio, & filii in paracleto,*
" *tres efficit cohærentes, alteram cum altero,* qui tres
" unum sunt." &c. *

By the above quotation from *Tertullian*, it may be
observed, that the same credit ought to be given to
this daring, bold, and untrue assertion of *Griesbach*,
as to Mr. *Porter*, when he affirms, that the pronouns
joined to God are all in the singular number.†

After

* Tertul. Adv. Prax.   † P. 12.

After what has been obſerved by Mr. *Porter,* concerning the words of our Saviour, *take, eat ;* [*] *this is my body :* I think it proper to confeſs myſelf a true Son of the Church of England, which with the primitive and ancient Church of Chriſt believe theſe words of our Saviour to be literally and ſpiritually true when he *ſaid unto them* THIS *is my blood of the new teſtament which is ſhed for many.*[†]—This was the new covenant which he made with his Diſciples, to them and to all that ſhould have Faith in him and his blood.—I think this is properly explained in our catechiſm, which informs us that the body and blood of Chriſt are *verily* and *indeed* taken and received, *ſpiritually,* by the *faithful* in the Lord's ſupper.—Had I not Faith to believe theſe words of Chriſt, I ſhould be fearful left I ſhould be one of thoſe that St. Paul tells us *eateth and drinketh unworthily,* not diſcerning *the Lord's body ;*[‡] which body as it is *ſpiritually* there, can be diſcerned *by Faith only.*

The denying the bread and wine, after conſecration, to contain the body and blood of Chriſt, and received, *by the faithful,* in the Lord's ſupper, was an hereſy that did not trouble the church, till the great improvements in the ſixteenth century ; when a *ſect* ſprung up who were denominated *Sacramentarians.* This was the period alſo when *Socinus* lived, the founder of Socinianiſm—A period when every one formed his own religion according as his own idol, *reaſon,*

[*] Matth. xxvi. 26. [†] Mark xiv. 22, 23, 24. [‡] 1 Cor. xi. 29.

reafon, directed; and many of them thought themfelves *fincere believers* by fo doing; but, I think it
was referved for the *charitable* and *humane* Mr. *Porter,*
to affert that, the opinion of the Chriflian Church
for the firft fifteen centuries " fhould be rejected
" *with abhorrence,*" as well as the words of Chrift.
To be fure, had *his zeal* againft the *Godhead* of our
Saviour and the fcriptures, been lefs violent, fome
of his readers would have perufed his Letter with
more pleafuie, and would have liked it full as well.

Mr. *Porter* tells Dr. *Hawker,*† that from " the
" *vague manner* in which you exprefs yourfelf on the
" *firft proof,* I have brought in fupport of the above
" obfervations of the miracle which is related in the
" hiftory of *Jofhua,* I know not whether you believe
" that the fun moves round the earth, or that the
" earth revolves upon its axis.—If the former be
" your opinion, I fhall moft certainly leave you in
" the undifturbed poffeffion of it.—If the latter, you
" *do not,* any more than *myfelf,* believe every *private*
" opinion of the writers of the Old and New Tefta-
" ment."

Mr. *Porter* here *exults* and thinks that he has pro-
duced a text of fcripture which contradicts the
known laws of nature, and that he has got Dr.
Hawker in a *dilemma;* that either he muft give up
the truth of the fcripture, or elfe muft believe what
is contrary to the laws of nature, viz. that the fcripture

ture afferts that the fun goes round the earth, and not the earth round the fun ;—but, *how will he find himfelf* ! when it is made to appear this text does not contradict the known laws of nature, but is quite a defcription of them, and that this famous text, on which he triumphs fo much, has nothing to do with the motion either of the fun or the earth.—Was he able to examine the original Hebrew he would find neither the fun or earth are there faid to move.—It only informs us that the *light proceeding from the fun,* and *the light proceeding from the moon* were made to be ftill, and to remain *preternaturally* upon *Gibeon* and *Ajalon,* until the Children of Ifrael had avenged themfelves on their enemies.—This was certainly a great miracle !—The light from the fun and moon was *ftill,* did not move off from thefe places a whole day ; which, (as the fcriptures defcribe it) was whilft the terraqueous globe made one revolution on its axis, (which is the meafure of a natural day in the firft chapter of Genefis) that is, whilft every part of the earth enjoyed an evening and a morning, twenty-four hours :—Thus, as the Hiftorian informs us, there was no day before this, neither will there be any after like it.*——Mr *Porter* goes on by telling us " that the ~~prophets~~ *Jofephus* are now allowed to be erro-" neous ; thus, fays he. the fun is reprefented (in " the Englifh Bible) as running a race," † but, *in the original it is not fo* ; the Hebrew word here tranflated

* See p. 19, 20. † Mr. Porter's Letter p. 39.

tranflated *fun*, as has been already obferved, does not fignify the body of the fun, but the *folar light* fent out from it.*—According to this pfalm, the Heavens declare the glory of God, &c. and are the material agents of this fyftem.—The *folar light* is here compared to a ftrong man running a race— "For," fays the Pfalmift, "in them *(the Heavens)* he "has fet a tabernacle or place for the fun *(Hebrew "folar light) going out from the body of the fun)* his go- "ing forth is from the end of Heaven, and his *cir- "cuit* to the ends of it, and there is nothing or place "hid from the heat thereof."—Many learned men have thought that this pfalm gives a moft beautiful defcription of nature and the material heavens, and not an erroneous one, as Mr. *Porter* afferts !

After this he goes on pointing out the errors to be found in the fcripture, which, fays he, "reprefent "the *earth* or *world* as *founded on the fea, and eftablifhed* "*on the flood.*"||—Has he not read that Mofes! who, in defcribing the formation of this aqueous globe, tells us,‡ that the waters firft furrounded the earth, and that afterwards he ordered them to *one place,* that was within the fhell of the earth, and then that the dry land appeared.—Hence we are informed that there is an abyfs of waters, within the fhell of the earth, and that according to the fcriptures, *the earth is founded on the fea, and eftablifhed on the flood!*—If this had not been revealed by *Mofes,* it is the general opinion

---

* See p. 21, 23. || Mr. Porter, p. 39.   ‡ Gen. i. 9.

opinion of Naturalifts that it is fo !—Hence it looks as if Mr. *Porter* was deficient in the knowledge of *natural philofophy*, as well as the *original* fcriptures !

His next objection to the truth of the fcriptures is, "that the *dew* is there called the dew of *heaven*, "and is there reprefented as falling upon the ground, "as dropping from the clouds, from heaven.'*—It feems to appear from this objection of Mr. *Porter*, that he is ignorant of the meaning of the word *heavens*, as made ufe of in fcripture. The word *heavens* made ufe of here, as well as in other parts of fcripture, means the *material heavens*, (as may be obferved in Mofes's hiftory of the creation, where they are particularly defcribed) the fpace of which are filled with the *firmament*, the *expanfion* ; which reaches from the fun to the extremities of the material fyftem.†—Philofophers tell us that the dew is raifed by the *heat of the fun* expanding the watery particles from the earth, in form of fteam, till they become *fpecifically* lighter than the atmofphere, by the pieffure of which it is made to afcend to a certain height, higher or lower, according to the heat or cold of it, where it is condenfed again by the cold, till it becomes of more fpecific weight than the atmofphere, and then drops or defcends to the earth by its own gravity, and *drops from the clouds of heaven* to the earth.—Had he been a philofopher or careful obferver of this operation of nature, he would not

F   have

have objeincluded to the truth of the fcripture on this
account, but found that the *dew* of *heaven* drops to
the ground from the clouds of *heaven*, and that nature confiims the defcription given of it in fcripture.

Mr. *Porter* in his reply to Dr. *Hawker* makes a-
nother attack on Ifaiah ix. 6. which he feems to dif-
like much, and in order to get rid of it, fays, " it is
" *highly probable* that the original text is corrupted,
" and that the *original* Hebrew would admit of a
" tranflation in perfeinct confiftency with *Unitarian*
" principles, (which tranflation fays he to Dr.
" *Hawker*) I am perfuaded, you have it not in your
" power to fet afide."*—It may be obferved that
he does not point out the corrupted part, neither
how it may be tranflated in perfeinct confiftency with
Unitarian principles!—If Mr. *Porter* does not underftand the *original Hebrew,* as it does not appear
that he docs, what affurance muft he have to tell us
that it will admit of a different tranflation, &c.!—
Did he underftand the Hebrew language he would
find, that the Englifh tranflation of this verfe, is a
very literal one from the original!†

In my remarks on Mr. *Porter's* Defence, I think
in pages 15, 16, 17, he will find a fufficient anfwer
to this fecond objeinction to this text; but left he
fhould ovcilook it, I will again give him a recapi-
tulation of it.

The words tranflated **mighty God,** in the Hebrew
fignifies

* Reply p. 18.   † See p. 15, 16, 17.

fignifies the great and mighty God, and the Hebrew word אל EL, which is the word for God, is
not applied to Kings, Magiftrates, &c. but to the
fecond perfon in the Effence—the very name that
the man Chrift invoked when his God forfook him
on the crofs.—Thus as Ifaiah informs us in this pro-
phecy, "unto us a Child is born, unto us a Son is
" given, and the government fhall be on his fhoulder,
" and his NAME fhall be called Wonderful, Coun-
" feller, the MIGHTY GOD, the everlafting FA-
" THER, the Prince of Peace." And he further
tells us,* that the fign which the Lord will give of
his coming fhall be "behold THE VIRGIN fhall
" conceive and bear a fon, and fhall call his name
" *Immanuel*,"—that is in the Hebrew—the God EL
with us.

Notwithftanding the above obfervations, we may
conclude, that though Mr. *Porter* will not allow
what he has afferted to be erroneous, yet it fhews
that he is unfettled in his opinion on the fcripture,
for he concludes by faying, " that all that I *can pre-*
" *fume to fay is* that *I believe* I am right ; if I fhould
" be miftaken in my opinion, confcious to myfelf
" that I have acted the upright part, by doing every
" thing in my power to come to the knowledge of
" the truth, I can place my confidence in a righte-
" ous and merciful Judge, as to be perfuaded that
" he

* Ifa, vii. 14.——See p. 8.

" he will make every allowance for thofe *unavoidable*
" *prejudices* under which I may have laboured."

Well, fays St. Paul,† *becaufe of* unbelief *they were*
broken off, and *thou ftandeth by* Faith—*be not* high-
minded *but fear.*

After this confeffion, which we hope may be fincere, we ought to join with him in prayer to *Je-*
hovah Elohim, our Lord God, that he will fend him
fpiritual affiftance to overcome his *prejudices,* and that
he will *grant him power* to read, learn, and inwardly
digeft all holy fcriptures, and that by patience and
comfort of the holy word, he may embrace and
ever hold faft the bleffed hope of everlafting life,
by a *true Faith* in our Saviour Jefus Chrift. *Amen.*

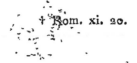

† Rom. xi. 20.

F I N I S.

Lightning Source UK Ltd.
Milton Keynes UK
UKHW02n2208130618
324210UK00007B/194/P